Social Media By The Minute

Laura De La Cruz

For information, contact
Laura De La Cruz
75 County Road A074
Chaparral, NM 88081
socialmediabytheminute@gmail.com

How to use this Workbook

You are a typical small business owner – hard-working and stretched thin. You are constantly told that you need to "do social media," yet you don't have the time to spare for one more "thing" to do!

This Workbook is designed to help you "do social media" but on your timeframe. It is broken down into 5 minute increments – if you have 5 minutes in a day, start there. If you have 10 minutes, you will take it to the next level, 15 minutes, the next level and so on. The goal is 30 minutes per day on social media for maximum impact on your business. The breakdown looks like this:

5 minutes – Ratings and Reviews Sites,

10 minutes – Facebook (plus R&R Sites),

15 minutes – Twitter (plus FB and R&R Sites),

20 minutes – LinkedIn (plus Twitter, FB and R&R),

25 minutes – Pinterest (plus the above),

30 minutes – Periscope (plus the above)

There are 6 workbook pages per weekday with tips and suggestions, as well as a place to note your activities. You are provided with a month's worth of worksheets. Use as needed!

Monday

Best Practices Daily Tip:

After downloading Periscope on your smart phone (and connecting it to your Twitter account), find at least 5 people to follow. Watching their broadcasts can help you determine what types of broadcasts you want to do! Remember, you never actually have to be on camera – you can record your surroundings instead, so don't be afraid to start!

5 Minutes

Date: _____

Rating and Review sites to check:

Yelp – yelp.com
Google+ Local –
google.com/+/learnmore/local
Superpages – superpages.com
Foursquare – foursquare.com
Manta – manta.com

Check these sites daily – are there ratings
and reviews? If so, be sure to address
them! Answer questions, respond to
negative comments, thank those that make
positive comments.

Track your work here:

_____
_____
_____
_____
_____
_____
_____
_____
_____
_____

10 Minutes

Facebook:

Best time to post: Saturdays @ noon (EST)
Post 3-1: 3 posts for engagement, 1 for promotion
Try to post 2-3 times per week
Post photos – they get the most "likes"
Use your logo for your picture photo, change your timeline photo regularly

Try to take five minutes each day to check your Facebook business page. Engage with people – respond! Address any negative comments or concerns. Thank those who post positive comments or reviews. Answer questions.

Track your work here:

_____

_____

_____

_____

_____

_____

_____

_____

_____

_____

15 Minutes

Twitter:

Tweet midweek & weekends around 12 & 6pm (EST)
Tweet 3-1: 3 tweets for engagement, 1 for promotion
Try to tweet every other day
Retweet and hashtag
Consider using coupons (twtqpon.com)

Try to take five minutes each day to tweet. Find local people to follow (customers, media, etc.) – use the search feature to find people in your zip code, city, county and industry. Consider connecting your Twitter account with your Facebook account so Tweets appear on FB.
Track your work here:

_____
_____
_____
_____
_____
_____
_____
_____
_____
_____
_____

20 Minutes

LinkedIn:

LinkedIn is about connections – fill out your profile and company page thoroughly
Try to update at least weekly
Spotlight products and services
Ask for recommendations and reciprocate
Join groups and engage in discussions
Make connections carefully – ask customers/clients if you can connect

Try to take five minutes each day to update. There is a little checkbox at the bottom of your "Share an update" box that copies everything you share with your Connections on Twitter. Use #in in Tweets to have them appear on LinkedIn.
Track your work here:

_____

_____

_____

_____

_____

_____

_____

_____

_____

_____

25 Minutes

Pinterest:

Pin original material or repin daily if possible
Best times are lunchtime, dinner time,
Saturday morning
Follow others and their boards
Pin/repin things that compliment your brand
and season
Link pins back to your website or include that
info in the pin

Try to take five minutes each day to pin.
Add pin descriptions. It can be up to 500
characters and should include SEO-friendly
keywords. You can also use hashtags
(sparingly).

Track your work here:

_____
_____
_____
_____
_____
_____
_____
_____
_____
_____

30 Minutes

Periscope:

Periscope is a live video-streaming app on your phone that posts your videos (for 24 hours) on Twitter and Periscope
Periscope followers are notified of your broadcasts and notification is posted to your Twitter feed
Use daily if possible for spontaneous (very short) broadcasts

Try to take five minutes each day to broadcast. Viewers can ask questions (you can respond) and give love (boosts your ratings). Broadcast anything! Engage!

Track your work here:

_____

_____

_____

_____

_____

_____

_____

_____

_____

_____

Tuesday

Best Practices Daily Tip:

Videos are King these days on Facebook and Facebook really, really likes those videos uploaded directly to them (not to YouTube or elsewhere and then linked to your page). Reports are engagement increases significantly with these as they play automatically whenever someone visits their news feed.

5 Minutes

Rating and Review sites to check:

Yelp – yelp.com
Google+ Local –
google.com/+/learnmore/local
Superpages – superpages.com
Foursquare – foursquare.com
Manta – manta.com

Check these sites daily – are there ratings and reviews? If so, be sure to address them! Answer questions, respond to negative comments, thank those that make positive comments.

Track your work here:

_____

_____

_____

_____

_____

_____

_____

_____

_____

_____

10 Minutes

Date: _____

Facebook:

Best time to post: Saturdays @ noon (EST)
Post 3-1: 3 posts for engagement, 1 for promotion
Try to post 2-3 times per week
Post photos – they get the most "likes"
Use your logo for your picture photo, change your timeline photo regularly

Try to take five minutes each day to check your Facebook business page. Engage with people – respond! Address any negative comments or concerns. Thank those who post positive comments or reviews. Answer questions.

Track your work here:

_____
_____
_____
_____
_____
_____
_____
_____
_____
_____
_____

15 Minutes

Date: _____

Twitter:

Tweet midweek & weekends around 12 & 6pm (EST)

Tweet 3-1: 3 tweets for engagement, 1 for promotion

Try to tweet every other day

Retweet and hashtag

Consider using coupons (twtqpon.com)

Try to take five minutes each day to tweet. Find local people to follow (customers, media, etc.) – use the search feature to find people in your zip code, city, county and industry. Consider connecting your Twitter account with your Facebook account so Tweets appear on FB.

Track your work here:

_____

_____

_____

_____

_____

_____

_____

_____

_____

_____

20 Minutes

LinkedIn:

LinkedIn is about connections – fill out your profile and company page thoroughly
Try to update at least weekly
Spotlight products and services
Ask for recommendations and reciprocate
Join groups and engage in discussions
Make connections carefully – ask customers/clients if you can connect

Try to take five minutes each day to update. There is a little checkbox at the bottom of your "Share an update" box that copies everything you share with your Connections on Twitter. Use #in in Tweets to have them appear on LinkedIn.
Track your work here:

_____

_____

_____

_____

_____

_____

_____

_____

_____

_____

25 Minutes

Pinterest:

Pin original material or repin daily if possible
Best times are lunchtime, dinner time,
Saturday morning
Follow others and their boards
Pin/repin things that compliment your brand
and season
Link pins back to your website or include that
info in the pin

Try to take five minutes each day to pin.
Add pin descriptions. It can be up to 500
characters and should include SEO-friendly
keywords. You can also use hashtags
(sparingly).

Track your work here:

_____

_____

_____

_____

_____

_____

_____

_____

_____

_____

30 Minutes

Periscope:

Periscope is a live video-streaming app on your phone that posts your videos (for 24 hours) on Twitter and Periscope
Periscope followers are notified of your broadcasts and notification is posted to your Twitter feed
Use daily if possible for spontaneous (very short) broadcasts

Try to take five minutes each day to broadcast. Viewers can ask questions (you can respond) and give love (boosts your ratings). Broadcast anything! Engage!

Track your work here:

_____
_____
_____
_____
_____
_____
_____
_____
_____
_____
_____

Wednesday

Best Practices Daily Tip:

Pinterest is all about the boards – create boards that are relevant to your products and/or services. You don't need a bunch at the beginning (3-4 is a good start) but try for those that capture the essence of what you do.

5 Minutes

Date: _____

Rating and Review sites to check:

Yelp – yelp.com
Google+ Local –
google.com/+/learnmore/local
Superpages – superpages.com
Foursquare – foursquare.com
Manta – manta.com

Check these sites daily – are there ratings
and reviews? If so, be sure to address
them! Answer questions, respond to
negative comments, thank those that make
positive comments.

Track your work here:

_____

_____

_____

_____

_____

_____

_____

_____

_____

_____

_____

10 Minutes

Facebook:

Best time to post: Saturdays @ noon (EST)
Post 3-1: 3 posts for engagement, 1 for promotion
Try to post 2-3 times per week
Post photos – they get the most "likes"
Use your logo for your picture photo, change your timeline photo regularly

Try to take five minutes each day to check your Facebook business page. Engage with people – respond! Address any negative comments or concerns. Thank those who post positive comments or reviews. Answer questions.

Track your work here:

_____

_____

_____

_____

_____

_____

_____

_____

_____

_____

15 Minutes

Twitter:

Tweet midweek & weekends around 12 & 6pm (EST)
Tweet 3-1: 3 tweets for engagement, 1 for promotion
Try to tweet every other day
Retweet and hashtag
Consider using coupons (twtqpon.com)

Try to take five minutes each day to tweet. Find local people to follow (customers, media, etc.) – use the search feature to find people in your zip code, city, county and industry. Consider connecting your Twitter account with your Facebook account so Tweets appear on FB.
Track your work here:

_____

_____

_____

_____

_____

_____

_____

_____

_____

_____

20 Minutes

LinkedIn:

LinkedIn is about connections – fill out your profile and company page thoroughly
Try to update at least weekly
Spotlight products and services
Ask for recommendations and reciprocate
Join groups and engage in discussions
Make connections carefully – ask customers/clients if you can connect

Try to take five minutes each day to update. There is a little checkbox at the bottom of your "Share an update" box that copies everything you share with your Connections on Twitter. Use #in in Tweets to have them appear on LinkedIn.
Track your work here:

_____

_____

_____

_____

_____

_____

_____

_____

_____

_____

25 Minutes

Pinterest:

Pin original material or repin daily if possible
Best times are lunchtime, dinner time,
Saturday morning
Follow others and their boards
Pin/repin things that compliment your brand
and season
Link pins back to your website or include that
info in the pin

Try to take five minutes each day to pin.
Add pin descriptions. It can be up to 500
characters and should include SEO-friendly
keywords. You can also use hashtags
(sparingly).

Track your work here:

_____
_____
_____
_____
_____
_____
_____
_____
_____
_____
_____

30 Minutes

Periscope:

Periscope is a live video-streaming app on your phone that posts your videos (for 24 hours) on Twitter and Periscope
Periscope followers are notified of your broadcasts and notification is posted to your Twitter feed
Use daily if possible for spontaneous (very short) broadcasts

Try to take five minutes each day to broadcast. Viewers can ask questions (you can respond) and give love (boosts your ratings). Broadcast anything! Engage!

Track your work here:

_____

_____

_____

_____

_____

_____

_____

_____

_____

_____

Thursday

Best Practices Daily Tip:

Tweets with one or two hashtags receive higher levels of engagement – just keep the hashtags relevant and avoid trendy (unless it is really relevant to your business and you can contribute to the discussion).

5 Minutes

Date: _____

Rating and Review sites to check:

Yelp – yelp.com
Google+ Local –
google.com/+/learnmore/local
Superpages – superpages.com
Foursquare – foursquare.com
Manta – manta.com

Check these sites daily – are there ratings
and reviews? If so, be sure to address
them! Answer questions, respond to
negative comments, thank those that make
positive comments.

Track your work here:

_____
_____
_____
_____
_____
_____
_____
_____
_____
_____

10 Minutes

Facebook:

Best time to post: Saturdays @ noon (EST)
Post 3-1: 3 posts for engagement, 1 for promotion
Try to post 2-3 times per week
Post photos – they get the most "likes"
Use your logo for your picture photo, change your timeline photo regularly

Try to take five minutes each day to check your Facebook business page. Engage with people – respond! Address any negative comments or concerns. Thank those who post positive comments or reviews. Answer questions.

Track your work here:

_____
_____
_____
_____
_____
_____
_____
_____
_____
_____
_____

15 Minutes

Twitter:

Tweet midweek & weekends around 12 & 6pm (EST)
Tweet 3-1: 3 tweets for engagement, 1 for promotion
Try to tweet every other day
Retweet and hashtag
Consider using coupons (twtqpon.com)

Try to take five minutes each day to tweet. Find local people to follow (customers, media, etc.) – use the search feature to find people in your zip code, city, county and industry. Consider connecting your Twitter account with your Facebook account so Tweets appear on FB.
Track your work here:

_____

_____

_____

_____

_____

_____

_____

_____

_____

_____

20 Minutes

LinkedIn:

LinkedIn is about connections – fill out your profile and company page thoroughly
Try to update at least weekly
Spotlight products and services
Ask for recommendations and reciprocate
Join groups and engage in discussions
Make connections carefully – ask customers/clients if you can connect

Try to take five minutes each day to update. There is a little checkbox at the bottom of your "Share an update" box that copies everything you share with your Connections on Twitter. Use #in in Tweets to have them appear on LinkedIn.
Track your work here:

_____
_____
_____
_____
_____
_____
_____
_____
_____
_____

25 Minutes

Pinterest:

Pin original material or repin daily if possible
Best times are lunchtime, dinner time,
Saturday morning
Follow others and their boards
Pin/repin things that compliment your brand
and season
Link pins back to your website or include that
info in the pin

Try to take five minutes each day to pin.
Add pin descriptions. It can be up to 500
characters and should include SEO-friendly
keywords. You can also use hashtags
(sparingly).

Track your work here:

_____
_____
_____
_____
_____
_____
_____
_____
_____
_____

30 Minutes

Periscope:

Periscope is a live video-streaming app on your phone that posts your videos (for 24 hours) on Twitter and Periscope
Periscope followers are notified of your broadcasts and notification is posted to your Twitter feed
Use daily if possible for spontaneous (very short) broadcasts

Try to take five minutes each day to broadcast. Viewers can ask questions (you can respond) and give love (boosts your ratings). Broadcast anything! Engage!

Track your work here:

_____

_____

_____

_____

_____

_____

_____

_____

_____

_____

Friday

Best Practices Daily Tip:

Make the most of your Facebook cover photo. It is the first thing people see when visiting your page. Make it interesting, appealing, professional, and change it regularly! Remember, each time you change your cover photo it puts an automatic update in the news feed.

5 Minutes

Rating and Review sites to check:

Yelp – yelp.com
Google+ Local –
google.com/+/learnmore/local
Superpages – superpages.com
Foursquare – foursquare.com
Manta – manta.com

Check these sites daily – are there ratings
and reviews? If so, be sure to address
them! Answer questions, respond to
negative comments, thank those that make
positive comments.

Track your work here:

_____

_____

_____

_____

_____

_____

_____

_____

_____

10 Minutes

Facebook:

Best time to post: Saturdays @ noon (EST)
Post 3-1: 3 posts for engagement, 1 for promotion
Try to post 2-3 times per week
Post photos – they get the most "likes"
Use your logo for your picture photo, change your timeline photo regularly

Try to take five minutes each day to check your Facebook business page. Engage with people – respond! Address any negative comments or concerns. Thank those who post positive comments or reviews. Answer questions.

Track your work here:

_____

_____

_____

_____

_____

_____

_____

_____

_____

_____

_____

15 Minutes

Twitter:

Tweet midweek & weekends around 12 & 6pm (EST)
Tweet 3-1: 3 tweets for engagement, 1 for promotion
Try to tweet every other day
Retweet and hashtag
Consider using coupons (twtqpon.com)

Try to take five minutes each day to tweet. Find local people to follow (customers, media, etc.) – use the search feature to find people in your zip code, city, county and industry. Consider connecting your Twitter account with your Facebook account so Tweets appear on FB.
Track your work here:

_____

_____

_____

_____

_____

_____

_____

_____

_____

20 Minutes

LinkedIn:

LinkedIn is about connections – fill out your profile and company page thoroughly
Try to update at least weekly
Spotlight products and services
Ask for recommendations and reciprocate
Join groups and engage in discussions
Make connections carefully – ask customers/clients if you can connect

Try to take five minutes each day to update. There is a little checkbox at the bottom of your "Share an update" box that copies everything you share with your Connections on Twitter. Use #in in Tweets to have them appear on LinkedIn.
Track your work here:

_____

_____

_____

_____

_____

_____

_____

_____

_____

_____

25 Minutes

Pinterest:

Pin original material or repin daily if possible
Best times are lunchtime, dinner time,
Saturday morning
Follow others and their boards
Pin/repin things that compliment your brand
and season
Link pins back to your website or include that
info in the pin

Try to take five minutes each day to pin.
Add pin descriptions. It can be up to 500
characters and should include SEO-friendly
keywords. You can also use hashtags
(sparingly).

Track your work here:

_____
_____
_____
_____
_____
_____
_____
_____
_____
_____
_____

30 Minutes

Periscope:

Periscope is a live video-streaming app on your phone that posts your videos (for 24 hours) on Twitter and Periscope
Periscope followers are notified of your broadcasts and notification is posted to your Twitter feed
Use daily if possible for spontaneous (very short) broadcasts

Try to take five minutes each day to broadcast. Viewers can ask questions (you can respond) and give love (boosts your ratings). Broadcast anything! Engage!

Track your work here:

_____
_____
_____
_____
_____
_____
_____
_____
_____
_____

30 Minutes

Periscope:

Periscope is a live video-streaming app on your phone that posts your videos (for 24 hours) on Twitter and Periscope
Periscope followers are notified of your broadcasts and notification is posted to your Twitter feed
Use daily if possible for spontaneous (very short) broadcasts

Try to take five minutes each day to broadcast. Viewers can ask questions (you can respond) and give love (boosts your ratings). Broadcast anything! Engage!

Track your work here:

_____

_____

_____

_____

_____

_____

_____

_____

_____

_____

30 Minutes

Periscope:

Periscope is a live video-streaming app on your phone that posts your videos (for 24 hours) on Twitter and Periscope
Periscope followers are notified of your broadcasts and notification is posted to your Twitter feed
Use daily if possible for spontaneous (very short) broadcasts

Try to take five minutes each day to broadcast. Viewers can ask questions (you can respond) and give love (boosts your ratings). Broadcast anything! Engage!

Track your work here:

_____

_____

_____

_____

_____

_____

_____

_____

_____

_____

Monday

Best Practices Daily Tip:

Never, never use all-caps in your posts. It SCREAMS amateur and is considered yelling in cyberspace. Unless of course, you really meant to yell!

5 Minutes

Date: _____

Rating and Review sites to check:

Yelp – yelp.com
Google+ Local –
google.com/+/learnmore/local
Superpages – superpages.com
Foursquare – foursquare.com
Manta – manta.com

Check these sites daily – are there ratings
and reviews? If so, be sure to address
them! Answer questions, respond to
negative comments, thank those that make
positive comments.

Track your work here:

_____

_____

_____

_____

_____

_____

_____

_____

_____

_____

10 Minutes

Date: _____

Facebook:

Best time to post: Saturdays @ noon (EST)
Post 3-1: 3 posts for engagement, 1 for promotion
Try to post 2-3 times per week
Post photos – they get the most "likes"
Use your logo for your picture photo, change your timeline photo regularly

Try to take five minutes each day to check your Facebook business page. Engage with people – respond! Address any negative comments or concerns. Thank those who post positive comments or reviews. Answer questions.

Track your work here:

_____
_____
_____
_____
_____
_____
_____
_____
_____
_____

15 Minutes

Twitter:

Tweet midweek & weekends around 12 & 6pm (EST)

Tweet 3-1: 3 tweets for engagement, 1 for promotion

Try to tweet every other day

Retweet and hashtag

Consider using coupons (twtqpon.com)

Try to take five minutes each day to tweet. Find local people to follow (customers, media, etc.) – use the search feature to find people in your zip code, city, county and industry. Consider connecting your Twitter account with your Facebook account so Tweets appear on FB.

Track your work here:

_____

_____

_____

_____

_____

_____

_____

_____

_____

20 Minutes

LinkedIn:

LinkedIn is about connections – fill out your
profile and company page thoroughly
Try to update at least weekly
Spotlight products and services
Ask for recommendations and reciprocate
Join groups and engage in discussions
Make connections carefully – ask
customers/clients if you can connect

Try to take five minutes each day to update.
There is a little checkbox at the bottom of
your "Share an update" box that copies
everything you share with your
Connections on Twitter. Use #in in Tweets
to have them appear on LinkedIn.
Track your work here:

_____
_____
_____
_____
_____
_____
_____
_____
_____
_____

25 Minutes

Pinterest:

Pin original material or repin daily if possible
Best times are lunchtime, dinner time,
Saturday morning
Follow others and their boards
Pin/repin things that compliment your brand
and season
Link pins back to your website or include that
info in the pin

Try to take five minutes each day to pin.
Add pin descriptions. It can be up to 500
characters and should include SEO-friendly
keywords. You can also use hashtags
(sparingly).

Track your work here:

_____

_____

_____

_____

_____

_____

_____

_____

_____

_____

30 Minutes

Periscope:

Periscope is a live video-streaming app on your phone that posts your videos (for 24 hours) on Twitter and Periscope
Periscope followers are notified of your broadcasts and notification is posted to your Twitter feed
Use daily if possible for spontaneous (very short) broadcasts

Try to take five minutes each day to broadcast. Viewers can ask questions (you can respond) and give love (boosts your ratings). Broadcast anything! Engage!

Track your work here:

_____
_____
_____
_____
_____
_____
_____
_____
_____
_____
_____

Tuesday

Best Practices Daily Tip:

If you aren't sure what to post on Facebook, remember these three tips :

1. make it familiar - this will resonate with fans

2. make it timely – stay current

3. make it novel – be original

5 Minutes

Date: _____

Rating and Review sites to check:

Yelp – yelp.com
Google+ Local –
google.com/+/learnmore/local
Superpages – superpages.com
Foursquare – foursquare.com
Manta – manta.com

Check these sites daily – are there ratings
and reviews? If so, be sure to address
them! Answer questions, respond to
negative comments, thank those that make
positive comments.

Track your work here:

_____
_____
_____
_____
_____
_____
_____
_____
_____
_____
_____

10 Minutes

Date: _____

Facebook:

Best time to post: Saturdays @ noon (EST)
Post 3-1: 3 posts for engagement, 1 for promotion
Try to post 2-3 times per week
Post photos – they get the most "likes"
Use your logo for your picture photo, change your timeline photo regularly

Try to take five minutes each day to check your Facebook business page. Engage with people – respond! Address any negative comments or concerns. Thank those who post positive comments or reviews. Answer questions.

Track your work here:

_____
_____
_____
_____
_____
_____
_____
_____
_____
_____

15 Minutes

Twitter:

Tweet midweek & weekends around 12 & 6pm (EST)
Tweet 3-1: 3 tweets for engagement, 1 for promotion
Try to tweet every other day
Retweet and hashtag
Consider using coupons (twtqpon.com)

Try to take five minutes each day to tweet. Find local people to follow (customers, media, etc.) – use the search feature to find people in your zip code, city, county and industry. Consider connecting your Twitter account with your Facebook account so Tweets appear on FB.
Track your work here:

_____
_____
_____
_____
_____
_____
_____
_____
_____
_____
_____

20 Minutes

LinkedIn:

LinkedIn is about connections – fill out your profile and company page thoroughly
Try to update at least weekly
Spotlight products and services
Ask for recommendations and reciprocate
Join groups and engage in discussions
Make connections carefully – ask customers/clients if you can connect

Try to take five minutes each day to update. There is a little checkbox at the bottom of your "Share an update" box that copies everything you share with your Connections on Twitter. Use #in in Tweets to have them appear on LinkedIn.
Track your work here:

_____

_____

_____

_____

_____

_____

_____

_____

_____

_____

25 Minutes

Pinterest:

Pin original material or repin daily if possible
Best times are lunchtime, dinner time,
Saturday morning
Follow others and their boards
Pin/repin things that compliment your brand
and season
Link pins back to your website or include that
info in the pin

Try to take five minutes each day to pin.
Add pin descriptions. It can be up to 500
characters and should include SEO-friendly
keywords. You can also use hashtags
(sparingly).

Track your work here:

_____

_____

_____

_____

_____

_____

_____

_____

_____

_____

_____

30 Minutes

Periscope:

Periscope is a live video-streaming app on your phone that posts your videos (for 24 hours) on Twitter and Periscope
Periscope followers are notified of your broadcasts and notification is posted to your Twitter feed
Use daily if possible for spontaneous (very short) broadcasts

Try to take five minutes each day to broadcast. Viewers can ask questions (you can respond) and give love (boosts your ratings). Broadcast anything! Engage!

Track your work here:

_____

_____

_____

_____

_____

_____

_____

_____

_____

_____

Wednesday

Best Practices Daily Tip:

Constantly build your LinkedIn connections, but not by pestering strangers. When you meet someone, ask if you can connect and then do so. Look at who your friends/family are connected to and ask if you can use their name for an introduction in order to connect with their connections.

5 Minutes

Rating and Review sites to check:

Yelp – yelp.com
Google+ Local –
google.com/+/learnmore/local
Superpages – superpages.com
Foursquare – foursquare.com
Manta – manta.com

Check these sites daily – are there ratings
and reviews? If so, be sure to address
them! Answer questions, respond to
negative comments, thank those that make
positive comments.

Track your work here:

_____
_____
_____
_____
_____
_____
_____
_____
_____
_____

10 Minutes

Date: _____

Facebook:

Best time to post: Saturdays @ noon (EST)
Post 3-1: 3 posts for engagement, 1 for promotion
Try to post 2-3 times per week
Post photos – they get the most "likes"
Use your logo for your picture photo, change your timeline photo regularly

Try to take five minutes each day to check your Facebook business page. Engage with people – respond! Address any negative comments or concerns. Thank those who post positive comments or reviews. Answer questions.

Track your work here:

_____
_____
_____
_____
_____
_____
_____
_____
_____
_____

15 Minutes

Twitter:

Tweet midweek & weekends around 12 & 6pm (EST)
Tweet 3-1: 3 tweets for engagement, 1 for promotion
Try to tweet every other day
Retweet and hashtag
Consider using coupons (twtqpon.com)

Try to take five minutes each day to tweet. Find local people to follow (customers, media, etc.) – use the search feature to find people in your zip code, city, county and industry. Consider connecting your Twitter account with your Facebook account so Tweets appear on FB.
Track your work here:

_____

_____

_____

_____

_____

_____

_____

_____

_____

_____

_____

20 Minutes

LinkedIn:

LinkedIn is about connections – fill out your profile and company page thoroughly
Try to update at least weekly
Spotlight products and services
Ask for recommendations and reciprocate
Join groups and engage in discussions
Make connections carefully – ask customers/clients if you can connect

Try to take five minutes each day to update. There is a little checkbox at the bottom of your "Share an update" box that copies everything you share with your Connections on Twitter. Use #in in Tweets to have them appear on LinkedIn.
Track your work here:

_____

_____

_____

_____

_____

_____

_____

_____

_____

_____

25 Minutes

Pinterest:

Pin original material or repin daily if possible
Best times are lunchtime, dinner time,
Saturday morning
Follow others and their boards
Pin/repin things that compliment your brand
and season
Link pins back to your website or include that
info in the pin

Try to take five minutes each day to pin.
Add pin descriptions. It can be up to 500
characters and should include SEO-friendly
keywords. You can also use hashtags
(sparingly).

Track your work here:

_____

_____

_____

_____

_____

_____

_____

_____

_____

_____

30 Minutes

Periscope:

Periscope is a live video-streaming app on your phone that posts your videos (for 24 hours) on Twitter and Periscope
Periscope followers are notified of your broadcasts and notification is posted to your Twitter feed
Use daily if possible for spontaneous (very short) broadcasts

Try to take five minutes each day to broadcast. Viewers can ask questions (you can respond) and give love (boosts your ratings). Broadcast anything! Engage!

Track your work here:

_____

_____

_____

_____

_____

_____

_____

_____

_____

_____

Thursday

Best Practices Daily Tip:

Use the Pinterest search function to find categories relevant to your business. Look for pins that are relevant to what you do and repin. Be sure to include a new note when you do with a link back to your webpage!

5 Minutes

Rating and Review sites to check:

Yelp – yelp.com
Google+ Local –
google.com/+/learnmore/local
Superpages – superpages.com
Foursquare – foursquare.com
Manta – manta.com

Check these sites daily – are there ratings
and reviews? If so, be sure to address
them! Answer questions, respond to
negative comments, thank those that make
positive comments.

Track your work here:

_____
_____
_____
_____
_____
_____
_____
_____
_____
_____

10 Minutes

Facebook:

Best time to post: Saturdays @ noon (EST)
Post 3-1: 3 posts for engagement, 1 for promotion
Try to post 2-3 times per week
Post photos – they get the most "likes"
Use your logo for your picture photo, change your timeline photo regularly

Try to take five minutes each day to check your Facebook business page. Engage with people – respond! Address any negative comments or concerns. Thank those who post positive comments or reviews. Answer questions.

Track your work here:

_____

_____

_____

_____

_____

_____

_____

_____

_____

_____

15 Minutes

Twitter:

Tweet midweek & weekends around 12 & 6pm (EST)

Tweet 3-1: 3 tweets for engagement, 1 for promotion

Try to tweet every other day

Retweet and hashtag

Consider using coupons (twtqpon.com)

Try to take five minutes each day to tweet. Find local people to follow (customers, media, etc.) – use the search feature to find people in your zip code, city, county and industry. Consider connecting your Twitter account with your Facebook account so Tweets appear on FB.

Track your work here:

_____

_____

_____

_____

_____

_____

_____

_____

_____

_____

20 Minutes

LinkedIn:

LinkedIn is about connections – fill out your profile and company page thoroughly
Try to update at least weekly
Spotlight products and services
Ask for recommendations and reciprocate
Join groups and engage in discussions
Make connections carefully – ask customers/clients if you can connect

Try to take five minutes each day to update. There is a little checkbox at the bottom of your "Share an update" box that copies everything you share with your Connections on Twitter. Use #in in Tweets to have them appear on LinkedIn.
Track your work here:

_____

_____

_____

_____

_____

_____

_____

_____

_____

_____

25 Minutes

Pinterest:

Pin original material or repin daily if possible
Best times are lunchtime, dinner time,
Saturday morning
Follow others and their boards
Pin/repin things that compliment your brand
and season
Link pins back to your website or include that
info in the pin

Try to take five minutes each day to pin.
Add pin descriptions. It can be up to 500
characters and should include SEO-friendly
keywords. You can also use hashtags
(sparingly).

Track your work here:

_____
_____
_____
_____
_____
_____
_____
_____
_____
_____

30 Minutes

Periscope:

Periscope is a live video-streaming app on your phone that posts your videos (for 24 hours) on Twitter and Periscope
Periscope followers are notified of your broadcasts and notification is posted to your Twitter feed
Use daily if possible for spontaneous (very short) broadcasts

Try to take five minutes each day to broadcast. Viewers can ask questions (you can respond) and give love (boosts your ratings). Broadcast anything! Engage!

Track your work here:

_____

_____

_____

_____

_____

_____

_____

_____

_____

_____

Friday

Best Practices Daily Tip:

In every post, include an CTA (call to action) – surprisingly enough, many people actually won't click on links (or call or email) unless you tell them to do so. Instructions help!

5 Minutes

Date: _____

Rating and Review sites to check:

Yelp – yelp.com
Google+ Local –
google.com/+/learnmore/local
Superpages – superpages.com
Foursquare – foursquare.com
Manta – manta.com

Check these sites daily – are there ratings and reviews? If so, be sure to address them! Answer questions, respond to negative comments, thank those that make positive comments.

Track your work here:

_____

_____

_____

_____

_____

_____

_____

_____

_____

_____

10 Minutes

Facebook:

Best time to post: Saturdays @ noon (EST)
Post 3-1: 3 posts for engagement, 1 for promotion
Try to post 2-3 times per week
Post photos – they get the most "likes"
Use your logo for your picture photo, change your timeline photo regularly

Try to take five minutes each day to check your Facebook business page. Engage with people – respond! Address any negative comments or concerns. Thank those who post positive comments or reviews. Answer questions.

Track your work here:

_____

_____

_____

_____

_____

_____

_____

_____

_____

_____

15 Minutes

Twitter:

Tweet midweek & weekends around 12 & 6pm (EST)

Tweet 3-1: 3 tweets for engagement, 1 for promotion

Try to tweet every other day

Retweet and hashtag

Consider using coupons (twtqpon.com)

Try to take five minutes each day to tweet. Find local people to follow (customers, media, etc.) – use the search feature to find people in your zip code, city, county and industry. Consider connecting your Twitter account with your Facebook account so Tweets appear on FB.

Track your work here:

_____

_____

_____

_____

_____

_____

_____

_____

_____

_____

20 Minutes   Date: _____

LinkedIn:

LinkedIn is about connections – fill out your
profile and company page thoroughly
Try to update at least weekly
Spotlight products and services
Ask for recommendations and reciprocate
Join groups and engage in discussions
Make connections carefully – ask
customers/clients if you can connect

Try to take five minutes each day to update.
There is a little checkbox at the bottom of
your "Share an update" box that copies
everything you share with your
Connections on Twitter. Use #in in Tweets
to have them appear on LinkedIn.
Track your work here:

_____

_____

_____

_____

_____

_____

_____

_____

_____

_____

_____

25 Minutes

Pinterest:

Pin original material or repin daily if possible
Best times are lunchtime, dinner time,
Saturday morning
Follow others and their boards
Pin/repin things that compliment your brand
and season
Link pins back to your website or include that
info in the pin

Try to take five minutes each day to pin.
Add pin descriptions. It can be up to 500
characters and should include SEO-friendly
keywords. You can also use hashtags
(sparingly).

Track your work here:

_____

_____

_____

_____

_____

_____

_____

_____

_____

30 Minutes

Periscope:

Periscope is a live video-streaming app on your phone that posts your videos (for 24 hours) on Twitter and Periscope

Periscope followers are notified of your broadcasts and notification is posted to your Twitter feed

Use daily if possible for spontaneous (very short) broadcasts

Try to take five minutes each day to broadcast. Viewers can ask questions (you can respond) and give love (boosts your ratings). Broadcast anything! Engage!

Track your work here:

_____

_____

_____

_____

_____

_____

_____

_____

_____

30 Minutes

Periscope:

Periscope is a live video-streaming app on your phone that posts your videos (for 24 hours) on Twitter and Periscope
Periscope followers are notified of your broadcasts and notification is posted to your Twitter feed
Use daily if possible for spontaneous (very short) broadcasts

Try to take five minutes each day to broadcast. Viewers can ask questions (you can respond) and give love (boosts your ratings). Broadcast anything! Engage!

Track your work here:

_____
_____
_____
_____
_____
_____
_____
_____
_____
_____
_____

30 Minutes

Periscope:

Periscope is a live video-streaming app on your phone that posts your videos (for 24 hours) on Twitter and Periscope
Periscope followers are notified of your broadcasts and notification is posted to your Twitter feed
Use daily if possible for spontaneous (very short) broadcasts

Try to take five minutes each day to broadcast. Viewers can ask questions (you can respond) and give love (boosts your ratings). Broadcast anything! Engage!

Track your work here:

_____

_____

_____

_____

_____

_____

_____

_____

_____

_____

Monday

Best Practices Daily Tip:

Publish on LinkedIn? Yes! Upload everything you have done and consider writing articles specifically for LinkedIn. Always include a call to action, particularly encouraging people to connect or reach out to you for assistance.

5 Minutes

Date: _____

Rating and Review sites to check:

Yelp – yelp.com
Google+ Local –
google.com/+/learnmore/local
Superpages – superpages.com
Foursquare – foursquare.com
Manta – manta.com

Check these sites daily – are there ratings and reviews? If so, be sure to address them! Answer questions, respond to negative comments, thank those that make positive comments.

Track your work here:

_____

_____

_____

_____

_____

_____

_____

_____

_____

_____

10 Minutes

Date: _____

Facebook:

Best time to post: Saturdays @ noon (EST)
Post 3-1: 3 posts for engagement, 1 for promotion
Try to post 2-3 times per week
Post photos – they get the most "likes"
Use your logo for your picture photo, change your timeline photo regularly

Try to take five minutes each day to check your Facebook business page. Engage with people – respond! Address any negative comments or concerns. Thank those who post positive comments or reviews. Answer questions.

Track your work here:

_____
_____
_____
_____
_____
_____
_____
_____
_____
_____

15 Minutes

Twitter:

Tweet midweek & weekends around 12 & 6pm (EST)

Tweet 3-1: 3 tweets for engagement, 1 for promotion

Try to tweet every other day

Retweet and hashtag

Consider using coupons (twtqpon.com)

Try to take five minutes each day to tweet. Find local people to follow (customers, media, etc.) – use the search feature to find people in your zip code, city, county and industry. Consider connecting your Twitter account with your Facebook account so Tweets appear on FB.

Track your work here:

_____

_____

_____

_____

_____

_____

_____

_____

_____

_____

20 Minutes   Date: _____

LinkedIn:

LinkedIn is about connections – fill out your
profile and company page thoroughly
Try to update at least weekly
Spotlight products and services
Ask for recommendations and reciprocate
Join groups and engage in discussions
Make connections carefully – ask
customers/clients if you can connect

Try to take five minutes each day to update.
There is a little checkbox at the bottom of
your "Share an update" box that copies
everything you share with your
Connections on Twitter. Use #in in Tweets
to have them appear on LinkedIn.
Track your work here:

_____

_____

_____

_____

_____

_____

_____

_____

_____

_____

25 Minutes   Date: _____

Pinterest:

Pin original material or repin daily if possible
Best times are lunchtime, dinner time,
Saturday morning
Follow others and their boards
Pin/repin things that compliment your brand
and season
Link pins back to your website or include that
info in the pin

Try to take five minutes each day to pin.
Add pin descriptions. It can be up to 500
characters and should include SEO-friendly
keywords. You can also use hashtags
(sparingly).

Track your work here:

_____

_____

_____

_____

_____

_____

_____

_____

_____

30 Minutes

Periscope:

Periscope is a live video-streaming app on your phone that posts your videos (for 24 hours) on Twitter and Periscope
Periscope followers are notified of your broadcasts and notification is posted to your Twitter feed
Use daily if possible for spontaneous (very short) broadcasts

Try to take five minutes each day to broadcast. Viewers can ask questions (you can respond) and give love (boosts your ratings). Broadcast anything! Engage!

Track your work here:

_____

_____

_____

_____

_____

_____

_____

_____

_____

_____

Tuesday

Best Practices Daily Tip:

If it fits your personality, be fun and quirky on Pinterest. Create a board that unique and engaging and people will follow. Remember, the audience on Pinterest is primarily female, so appeal to their values and aspirations.

5 Minutes

Date: _____

Rating and Review sites to check:

Yelp – yelp.com
Google+ Local –
google.com/+/learnmore/local
Superpages – superpages.com
Foursquare – foursquare.com
Manta – manta.com

Check these sites daily – are there ratings and reviews? If so, be sure to address them! Answer questions, respond to negative comments, thank those that make positive comments.

Track your work here:

_____
_____
_____
_____
_____
_____
_____
_____
_____
_____

10 Minutes

Facebook:

Best time to post: Saturdays @ noon (EST)
Post 3-1: 3 posts for engagement, 1 for promotion
Try to post 2-3 times per week
Post photos – they get the most "likes"
Use your logo for your picture photo, change your timeline photo regularly

Try to take five minutes each day to check your Facebook business page. Engage with people – respond! Address any negative comments or concerns. Thank those who post positive comments or reviews. Answer questions.

Track your work here:

_____

_____

_____

_____

_____

_____

_____

_____

_____

_____

_____

15 Minutes

Twitter:

Tweet midweek & weekends around 12 & 6pm (EST)
Tweet 3-1: 3 tweets for engagement, 1 for promotion
Try to tweet every other day
Retweet and hashtag
Consider using coupons (twtqpon.com)

Try to take five minutes each day to tweet. Find local people to follow (customers, media, etc.) – use the search feature to find people in your zip code, city, county and industry. Consider connecting your Twitter account with your Facebook account so Tweets appear on FB.
Track your work here:

_____
_____
_____
_____
_____
_____
_____
_____
_____
_____

20 Minutes

LinkedIn:

LinkedIn is about connections – fill out your profile and company page thoroughly
Try to update at least weekly
Spotlight products and services
Ask for recommendations and reciprocate
Join groups and engage in discussions
Make connections carefully – ask customers/clients if you can connect

Try to take five minutes each day to update. There is a little checkbox at the bottom of your "Share an update" box that copies everything you share with your Connections on Twitter. Use #in in Tweets to have them appear on LinkedIn.
Track your work here:

_____

_____

_____

_____

_____

_____

_____

_____

_____

_____

_____

25 Minutes

Pinterest:

Pin original material or repin daily if possible
Best times are lunchtime, dinner time,
Saturday morning
Follow others and their boards
Pin/repin things that compliment your brand
and season
Link pins back to your website or include that
info in the pin

Try to take five minutes each day to pin.
Add pin descriptions. It can be up to 500
characters and should include SEO-friendly
keywords. You can also use hashtags
(sparingly).

Track your work here:

_____
_____
_____
_____
_____
_____
_____
_____
_____
_____
_____

30 Minutes

Periscope:

Periscope is a live video-streaming app on your phone that posts your videos (for 24 hours) on Twitter and Periscope
Periscope followers are notified of your broadcasts and notification is posted to your Twitter feed
Use daily if possible for spontaneous (very short) broadcasts

Try to take five minutes each day to broadcast. Viewers can ask questions (you can respond) and give love (boosts your ratings). Broadcast anything! Engage!

Track your work here:

_____
_____
_____
_____
_____
_____
_____
_____
_____
_____
_____

Wednesday

Best Practices Daily Tip:

Pictures can help your Twitter feed stand out. So can video! With Periscope, you can have the broadcast added to your Twitter feed (for 24 hours). Add pictures and video to engage and build your following.

5 Minutes

Date: _____

Rating and Review sites to check:

Yelp – yelp.com
Google+ Local –
google.com/+/learnmore/local
Superpages – superpages.com
Foursquare – foursquare.com
Manta – manta.com

Check these sites daily – are there ratings
and reviews? If so, be sure to address
them! Answer questions, respond to
negative comments, thank those that make
positive comments.

Track your work here:

_____
_____
_____
_____
_____
_____
_____
_____
_____
_____

10 Minutes

Date: _____

Facebook:

Best time to post: Saturdays @ noon (EST)
Post 3-1: 3 posts for engagement, 1 for promotion
Try to post 2-3 times per week
Post photos – they get the most "likes"
Use your logo for your picture photo, change your timeline photo regularly

Try to take five minutes each day to check your Facebook business page. Engage with people – respond! Address any negative comments or concerns. Thank those who post positive comments or reviews. Answer questions.

Track your work here:

_____

_____

_____

_____

_____

_____

_____

_____

_____

15 Minutes

Date: _____

Twitter:

Tweet midweek & weekends around 12 & 6pm (EST)

Tweet 3-1: 3 tweets for engagement, 1 for promotion

Try to tweet every other day

Retweet and hashtag

Consider using coupons (twtqpon.com)

Try to take five minutes each day to tweet. Find local people to follow (customers, media, etc.) – use the search feature to find people in your zip code, city, county and industry. Consider connecting your Twitter account with your Facebook account so Tweets appear on FB.

Track your work here:

_____

_____

_____

_____

_____

_____

_____

_____

_____

_____

_____

20 Minutes

LinkedIn:

LinkedIn is about connections – fill out your profile and company page thoroughly
Try to update at least weekly
Spotlight products and services
Ask for recommendations and reciprocate
Join groups and engage in discussions
Make connections carefully – ask customers/clients if you can connect

Try to take five minutes each day to update. There is a little checkbox at the bottom of your "Share an update" box that copies everything you share with your Connections on Twitter. Use #in in Tweets to have them appear on LinkedIn.
Track your work here:

_____

_____

_____

_____

_____

_____

_____

_____

_____

_____

25 Minutes

Pinterest:

Pin original material or repin daily if possible
Best times are lunchtime, dinner time,
Saturday morning
Follow others and their boards
Pin/repin things that compliment your brand
and season
Link pins back to your website or include that
info in the pin

Try to take five minutes each day to pin.
Add pin descriptions. It can be up to 500
characters and should include SEO-friendly
keywords. You can also use hashtags
(sparingly).

Track your work here:

_____
_____
_____
_____
_____
_____
_____
_____
_____
_____

30 Minutes

Periscope:

Periscope is a live video-streaming app on your phone that posts your videos (for 24 hours) on Twitter and Periscope
Periscope followers are notified of your broadcasts and notification is posted to your Twitter feed
Use daily if possible for spontaneous (very short) broadcasts

Try to take five minutes each day to broadcast. Viewers can ask questions (you can respond) and give love (boosts your ratings). Broadcast anything! Engage!

Track your work here:

_____
_____
_____
_____
_____
_____
_____
_____
_____
_____

Thursday

Best Practices Daily Tip:

Highlight or pin your best posts on Facebook. The highlight option (done by selecting the star icon on the top right corner of your post) spreads the post across the width of your FB page, making it more visible. Pinning (pin to top) makes a post the first thing people see when coming to your page. Change this weekly for maximum engagement!

5 Minutes

Rating and Review sites to check:

Yelp – yelp.com
Google+ Local –
google.com/+/learnmore/local
Superpages – superpages.com
Foursquare – foursquare.com
Manta – manta.com

Check these sites daily – are there ratings
and reviews? If so, be sure to address
them! Answer questions, respond to
negative comments, thank those that make
positive comments.

Track your work here:

_____

_____

_____

_____

_____

_____

_____

_____

_____

_____

_____

10 Minutes

Facebook:

Best time to post: Saturdays @ noon (EST)
Post 3-1: 3 posts for engagement, 1 for
promotion
Try to post 2-3 times per week
Post photos – they get the most "likes"
Use your logo for your picture photo, change
your timeline photo regularly

Try to take five minutes each day to check
your Facebook business page. Engage with
people – respond! Address any negative
comments or concerns. Thank those who
post positive comments or reviews. Answer
questions.

Track your work here:

_____

_____

_____

_____

_____

_____

_____

_____

_____

_____

_____

15 Minutes

Twitter:

Tweet midweek & weekends around 12 & 6pm (EST)
Tweet 3-1: 3 tweets for engagement, 1 for promotion
Try to tweet every other day
Retweet and hashtag
Consider using coupons (twtqpon.com)

Try to take five minutes each day to tweet. Find local people to follow (customers, media, etc.) – use the search feature to find people in your zip code, city, county and industry. Consider connecting your Twitter account with your Facebook account so Tweets appear on FB.
Track your work here:

_____

_____

_____

_____

_____

_____

_____

_____

_____

20 Minutes

LinkedIn:

LinkedIn is about connections – fill out your profile and company page thoroughly
Try to update at least weekly
Spotlight products and services
Ask for recommendations and reciprocate
Join groups and engage in discussions
Make connections carefully – ask customers/clients if you can connect

Try to take five minutes each day to update. There is a little checkbox at the bottom of your "Share an update" box that copies everything you share with your Connections on Twitter. Use #in in Tweets to have them appear on LinkedIn.
Track your work here:

_____

_____

_____

_____

_____

_____

_____

_____

_____

_____

_____

25 Minutes

Pinterest:

Pin original material or repin daily if possible
Best times are lunchtime, dinner time,
Saturday morning
Follow others and their boards
Pin/repin things that compliment your brand
and season
Link pins back to your website or include that
info in the pin

Try to take five minutes each day to pin.
Add pin descriptions. It can be up to 500
characters and should include SEO-friendly
keywords. You can also use hashtags
(sparingly).

Track your work here:

_____

_____

_____

_____

_____

_____

_____

_____

_____

_____

30 Minutes

Periscope:

Periscope is a live video-streaming app on your phone that posts your videos (for 24 hours) on Twitter and Periscope
Periscope followers are notified of your broadcasts and notification is posted to your Twitter feed
Use daily if possible for spontaneous (very short) broadcasts

Try to take five minutes each day to broadcast. Viewers can ask questions (you can respond) and give love (boosts your ratings). Broadcast anything! Engage!

Track your work here:

_____
_____
_____
_____
_____
_____
_____
_____
_____
_____

Friday

Best Practices Daily Tip:

Use the status update area of LinkedIn to share information on your accomplishments. Use it to provide information to customers and clients, such as links to helpful articles or news.

5 Minutes

Rating and Review sites to check:

Yelp – yelp.com
Google+ Local –
google.com/+/learnmore/local
Superpages – superpages.com
Foursquare – foursquare.com
Manta – manta.com

Check these sites daily – are there ratings
and reviews? If so, be sure to address
them! Answer questions, respond to
negative comments, thank those that make
positive comments.

Track your work here:

_____
_____
_____
_____
_____
_____
_____
_____
_____
_____
_____

10 Minutes

Facebook:

Best time to post: Saturdays @ noon (EST)
Post 3-1: 3 posts for engagement, 1 for
promotion
Try to post 2-3 times per week
Post photos – they get the most "likes"
Use your logo for your picture photo, change
your timeline photo regularly

Try to take five minutes each day to check
your Facebook business page. Engage with
people – respond! Address any negative
comments or concerns. Thank those who
post positive comments or reviews. Answer
questions.

Track your work here:

_____
_____
_____
_____
_____
_____
_____
_____
_____
_____
_____

15 Minutes

Date: _____

Twitter:

Tweet midweek & weekends around 12 & 6pm (EST)

Tweet 3-1: 3 tweets for engagement, 1 for promotion

Try to tweet every other day

Retweet and hashtag

Consider using coupons (twtqpon.com)

Try to take five minutes each day to tweet. Find local people to follow (customers, media, etc.) – use the search feature to find people in your zip code, city, county and industry. Consider connecting your Twitter account with your Facebook account so Tweets appear on FB.

Track your work here:

_____

_____

_____

_____

_____

_____

_____

_____

_____

_____

_____

20 Minutes

LinkedIn:

LinkedIn is about connections – fill out your
profile and company page thoroughly
Try to update at least weekly
Spotlight products and services
Ask for recommendations and reciprocate
Join groups and engage in discussions
Make connections carefully – ask
customers/clients if you can connect

Try to take five minutes each day to update.
There is a little checkbox at the bottom of
your "Share an update" box that copies
everything you share with your
Connections on Twitter. Use #in in Tweets
to have them appear on LinkedIn.
Track your work here:

_____

_____

_____

_____

_____

_____

_____

_____

_____

_____

25 Minutes

Pinterest:

Pin original material or repin daily if possible
Best times are lunchtime, dinner time,
Saturday morning
Follow others and their boards
Pin/repin things that compliment your brand
and season
Link pins back to your website or include that
info in the pin

Try to take five minutes each day to pin.
Add pin descriptions. It can be up to 500
characters and should include SEO-friendly
keywords. You can also use hashtags
(sparingly).

Track your work here:

_____
_____
_____
_____
_____
_____
_____
_____
_____
_____
_____

30 Minutes

Periscope:

Periscope is a live video-streaming app on your phone that posts your videos (for 24 hours) on Twitter and Periscope
Periscope followers are notified of your broadcasts and notification is posted to your Twitter feed
Use daily if possible for spontaneous (very short) broadcasts

Try to take five minutes each day to broadcast. Viewers can ask questions (you can respond) and give love (boosts your ratings). Broadcast anything! Engage!

Track your work here:

_____
_____
_____
_____
_____
_____
_____
_____
_____
_____

30 Minutes

Periscope:

Periscope is a live video-streaming app on your phone that posts your videos (for 24 hours) on Twitter and Periscope
Periscope followers are notified of your broadcasts and notification is posted to your Twitter feed
Use daily if possible for spontaneous (very short) broadcasts

Try to take five minutes each day to broadcast. Viewers can ask questions (you can respond) and give love (boosts your ratings). Broadcast anything! Engage!

Track your work here:

_____
_____
_____
_____
_____
_____
_____
_____
_____
_____

30 Minutes

Periscope:

Periscope is a live video-streaming app on your phone that posts your videos (for 24 hours) on Twitter and Periscope
Periscope followers are notified of your broadcasts and notification is posted to your Twitter feed
Use daily if possible for spontaneous (very short) broadcasts

Try to take five minutes each day to broadcast. Viewers can ask questions (you can respond) and give love (boosts your ratings). Broadcast anything! Engage!

Track your work here:

_____

_____

_____

_____

_____

_____

_____

_____

_____

_____

Monday

Best Practices Daily Tip:

Got mentioned on Twitter? Retweet! Add a personalized note and you are now connecting!

5 Minutes

Date: _____

Rating and Review sites to check:

Yelp – yelp.com
Google+ Local –
google.com/+/learnmore/local
Superpages – superpages.com
Foursquare – foursquare.com
Manta – manta.com

Check these sites daily – are there ratings
and reviews? If so, be sure to address
them! Answer questions, respond to
negative comments, thank those that make
positive comments.

Track your work here:

_____
_____
_____
_____
_____
_____
_____
_____
_____
_____

10 Minutes

Date: _____

Facebook:

Best time to post: Saturdays @ noon (EST)
Post 3-1: 3 posts for engagement, 1 for promotion
Try to post 2-3 times per week
Post photos – they get the most "likes"
Use your logo for your picture photo, change your timeline photo regularly

Try to take five minutes each day to check your Facebook business page. Engage with people – respond! Address any negative comments or concerns. Thank those who post positive comments or reviews. Answer questions.

Track your work here:

_____
_____
_____
_____
_____
_____
_____
_____
_____
_____
_____

15 Minutes

Date: _____

Twitter:

Tweet midweek & weekends around 12 & 6pm (EST)
Tweet 3-1: 3 tweets for engagement, 1 for promotion
Try to tweet every other day
Retweet and hashtag
Consider using coupons (twtqpon.com)

Try to take five minutes each day to tweet. Find local people to follow (customers, media, etc.) – use the search feature to find people in your zip code, city, county and industry. Consider connecting your Twitter account with your Facebook account so Tweets appear on FB.
Track your work here:

_____

_____

_____

_____

_____

_____

_____

_____

_____

_____

20 Minutes

LinkedIn:

LinkedIn is about connections – fill out your profile and company page thoroughly
Try to update at least weekly
Spotlight products and services
Ask for recommendations and reciprocate
Join groups and engage in discussions
Make connections carefully – ask customers/clients if you can connect

Try to take five minutes each day to update. There is a little checkbox at the bottom of your "Share an update" box that copies everything you share with your Connections on Twitter. Use #in in Tweets to have them appear on LinkedIn.
Track your work here:

_____
_____
_____
_____
_____
_____
_____
_____
_____
_____

25 Minutes

Pinterest:

Pin original material or repin daily if possible
Best times are lunchtime, dinner time,
Saturday morning
Follow others and their boards
Pin/repin things that compliment your brand
and season
Link pins back to your website or include that
info in the pin

Try to take five minutes each day to pin.
Add pin descriptions. It can be up to 500
characters and should include SEO-friendly
keywords. You can also use hashtags
(sparingly).

Track your work here:

_____
_____
_____
_____
_____
_____
_____
_____
_____
_____

30 Minutes

Date: _____

Periscope:

Periscope is a live video-streaming app on your phone that posts your videos (for 24 hours) on Twitter and Periscope

Periscope followers are notified of your broadcasts and notification is posted to your Twitter feed

Use daily if possible for spontaneous (very short) broadcasts

Try to take five minutes each day to broadcast. Viewers can ask questions (you can respond) and give love (boosts your ratings). Broadcast anything! Engage!

Track your work here:

_____

_____

_____

_____

_____

_____

_____

_____

_____

_____

Tuesday

Best Practices Daily Tip:

Share interesting content! No one wants to see a Facebook page or Pinterest page that is just one big sales pitch! By offering interesting content, you build awareness and community.

5 Minutes

Rating and Review sites to check:

Yelp – yelp.com
Google+ Local –
google.com/+/learnmore/local
Superpages – superpages.com
Foursquare – foursquare.com
Manta – manta.com

Check these sites daily – are there ratings
and reviews? If so, be sure to address
them! Answer questions, respond to
negative comments, thank those that make
positive comments.

Track your work here:

_____
_____
_____
_____
_____
_____
_____
_____
_____
_____
_____

10 Minutes

Facebook:

Best time to post: Saturdays @ noon (EST)
Post 3-1: 3 posts for engagement, 1 for
promotion
Try to post 2-3 times per week
Post photos – they get the most "likes"
Use your logo for your picture photo, change
your timeline photo regularly

Try to take five minutes each day to check
your Facebook business page. Engage with
people – respond! Address any negative
comments or concerns. Thank those who
post positive comments or reviews. Answer
questions.

Track your work here:

_____
_____
_____
_____
_____
_____
_____
_____
_____
_____

15 Minutes

Twitter:

Tweet midweek & weekends around 12 & 6pm (EST)
Tweet 3-1: 3 tweets for engagement, 1 for promotion
Try to tweet every other day
Retweet and hashtag
Consider using coupons (twtqpon.com)

Try to take five minutes each day to tweet. Find local people to follow (customers, media, etc.) – use the search feature to find people in your zip code, city, county and industry. Consider connecting your Twitter account with your Facebook account so Tweets appear on FB.
Track your work here:

_____

_____

_____

_____

_____

_____

_____

_____

_____

_____

20 Minutes

LinkedIn:

LinkedIn is about connections – fill out your profile and company page thoroughly
Try to update at least weekly
Spotlight products and services
Ask for recommendations and reciprocate
Join groups and engage in discussions
Make connections carefully – ask customers/clients if you can connect

Try to take five minutes each day to update. There is a little checkbox at the bottom of your "Share an update" box that copies everything you share with your Connections on Twitter. Use #in in Tweets to have them appear on LinkedIn.
Track your work here:

_____

_____

_____

_____

_____

_____

_____

_____

_____

_____

25 Minutes

Pinterest:

Pin original material or repin daily if possible
Best times are lunchtime, dinner time,
Saturday morning
Follow others and their boards
Pin/repin things that compliment your brand
and season
Link pins back to your website or include that
info in the pin

Try to take five minutes each day to pin.
Add pin descriptions. It can be up to 500
characters and should include SEO-friendly
keywords. You can also use hashtags
(sparingly).

Track your work here:

_____

_____

_____

_____

_____

_____

_____

_____

_____

_____

_____

30 Minutes

Periscope:

Periscope is a live video-streaming app on your phone that posts your videos (for 24 hours) on Twitter and Periscope

Periscope followers are notified of your broadcasts and notification is posted to your Twitter feed

Use daily if possible for spontaneous (very short) broadcasts

Try to take five minutes each day to broadcast. Viewers can ask questions (you can respond) and give love (boosts your ratings). Broadcast anything! Engage!

Track your work here:

_____
_____
_____
_____
_____
_____
_____
_____
_____
_____
_____

Wednesday

Best Practices Daily Tip:

Use all forms of social media to thank your customers and fans. Pick someone randomly and give them a shout-out. Take time to thank people and you will be rewarded!

5 Minutes

Date: _____

Rating and Review sites to check:

Yelp – yelp.com
Google+ Local –
google.com/+/learnmore/local
Superpages – superpages.com
Foursquare – foursquare.com
Manta – manta.com

Check these sites daily – are there ratings
and reviews? If so, be sure to address
them! Answer questions, respond to
negative comments, thank those that make
positive comments.

Track your work here:

_____
_____
_____
_____
_____
_____
_____
_____
_____
_____

10 Minutes

Date: _____

Facebook:

Best time to post: Saturdays @ noon (EST)
Post 3-1: 3 posts for engagement, 1 for promotion
Try to post 2-3 times per week
Post photos – they get the most "likes"
Use your logo for your picture photo, change your timeline photo regularly

Try to take five minutes each day to check your Facebook business page. Engage with people – respond! Address any negative comments or concerns. Thank those who post positive comments or reviews. Answer questions.

Track your work here:

_____
_____
_____
_____
_____
_____
_____
_____
_____
_____
_____

15 Minutes

Twitter:

Tweet midweek & weekends around 12 & 6pm (EST)
Tweet 3-1: 3 tweets for engagement, 1 for promotion
Try to tweet every other day
Retweet and hashtag
Consider using coupons (twtqpon.com)

Try to take five minutes each day to tweet. Find local people to follow (customers, media, etc.) – use the search feature to find people in your zip code, city, county and industry. Consider connecting your Twitter account with your Facebook account so Tweets appear on FB.
Track your work here:

_____

_____

_____

_____

_____

_____

_____

_____

_____

_____

20 Minutes

LinkedIn:

LinkedIn is about connections – fill out your profile and company page thoroughly
Try to update at least weekly
Spotlight products and services
Ask for recommendations and reciprocate
Join groups and engage in discussions
Make connections carefully – ask customers/clients if you can connect

Try to take five minutes each day to update. There is a little checkbox at the bottom of your "Share an update" box that copies everything you share with your Connections on Twitter. Use #in in Tweets to have them appear on LinkedIn.
Track your work here:

_____

_____

_____

_____

_____

_____

_____

_____

_____

_____

25 Minutes

Pinterest:

Pin original material or repin daily if possible
Best times are lunchtime, dinner time,
Saturday morning
Follow others and their boards
Pin/repin things that compliment your brand
and season
Link pins back to your website or include that
info in the pin

Try to take five minutes each day to pin.
Add pin descriptions. It can be up to 500
characters and should include SEO-friendly
keywords. You can also use hashtags
(sparingly).

Track your work here:

_____

_____

_____

_____

_____

_____

_____

_____

_____

_____

30 Minutes

Periscope:

Periscope is a live video-streaming app on your phone that posts your videos (for 24 hours) on Twitter and Periscope
Periscope followers are notified of your broadcasts and notification is posted to your Twitter feed
Use daily if possible for spontaneous (very short) broadcasts

Try to take five minutes each day to broadcast. Viewers can ask questions (you can respond) and give love (boosts your ratings). Broadcast anything! Engage!

Track your work here:

_____
_____
_____
_____
_____
_____
_____
_____
_____
_____

Thursday

Best Practices Daily Tip:

You do need to get "found" on Pinterest. Do that by repinning, liking, and commenting. Repins, likes and follows trigger emails to those people, who may then check out your Boards and follow you.

5 Minutes

Date: _____

Rating and Review sites to check:

Yelp – yelp.com
Google+ Local –
google.com/+/learnmore/local
Superpages – superpages.com
Foursquare – foursquare.com
Manta – manta.com

Check these sites daily – are there ratings and reviews? If so, be sure to address them! Answer questions, respond to negative comments, thank those that make positive comments.

Track your work here:

_____
_____
_____
_____
_____
_____
_____
_____
_____
_____
_____

10 Minutes   Date: _____

Facebook:

Best time to post: Saturdays @ noon (EST)
Post 3-1: 3 posts for engagement, 1 for promotion
Try to post 2-3 times per week
Post photos – they get the most "likes"
Use your logo for your picture photo, change your timeline photo regularly

Try to take five minutes each day to check your Facebook business page. Engage with people – respond! Address any negative comments or concerns. Thank those who post positive comments or reviews. Answer questions.

Track your work here:

_____
_____
_____
_____
_____
_____
_____
_____
_____
_____
_____

15 Minutes

Twitter:

Tweet midweek & weekends around 12 & 6pm (EST)
Tweet 3-1: 3 tweets for engagement, 1 for promotion
Try to tweet every other day
Retweet and hashtag
Consider using coupons (twtqpon.com)

Try to take five minutes each day to tweet. Find local people to follow (customers, media, etc.) – use the search feature to find people in your zip code, city, county and industry. Consider connecting your Twitter account with your Facebook account so Tweets appear on FB.
Track your work here:

_____

_____

_____

_____

_____

_____

_____

_____

_____

_____

_____

20 Minutes

LinkedIn:

LinkedIn is about connections – fill out your profile and company page thoroughly
Try to update at least weekly
Spotlight products and services
Ask for recommendations and reciprocate
Join groups and engage in discussions
Make connections carefully – ask customers/clients if you can connect

Try to take five minutes each day to update. There is a little checkbox at the bottom of your "Share an update" box that copies everything you share with your Connections on Twitter. Use #in in Tweets to have them appear on LinkedIn.
Track your work here:

_____
_____
_____
_____
_____
_____
_____
_____
_____
_____

25 Minutes

Pinterest:

Pin original material or repin daily if possible
Best times are lunchtime, dinner time,
Saturday morning
Follow others and their boards
Pin/repin things that compliment your brand
and season
Link pins back to your website or include that
info in the pin

Try to take five minutes each day to pin.
Add pin descriptions. It can be up to 500
characters and should include SEO-friendly
keywords. You can also use hashtags
(sparingly).

Track your work here:

_____
_____
_____
_____
_____
_____
_____
_____
_____
_____

30 Minutes

Periscope:

Periscope is a live video-streaming app on your phone that posts your videos (for 24 hours) on Twitter and Periscope
Periscope followers are notified of your broadcasts and notification is posted to your Twitter feed
Use daily if possible for spontaneous (very short) broadcasts

Try to take five minutes each day to broadcast. Viewers can ask questions (you can respond) and give love (boosts your ratings). Broadcast anything! Engage!

Track your work here:

_____
_____
_____
_____
_____
_____
_____
_____
_____
_____
_____

Friday

Best Practices Daily Tip:

Make sure you have social media buttons on your website so visitors can "one-click" to follow you. You can even set up your Facebook button to generate an automatic "like" for your page. Check the links regularly to make sure they work.

5 Minutes

Date: _____

Rating and Review sites to check:

Yelp – yelp.com
Google+ Local –
google.com/+/learnmore/local
Superpages – superpages.com
Foursquare – foursquare.com
Manta – manta.com

Check these sites daily – are there ratings
and reviews? If so, be sure to address
them! Answer questions, respond to
negative comments, thank those that make
positive comments.

Track your work here:

_____
_____
_____
_____
_____
_____
_____
_____
_____
_____
_____

10 Minutes

Date: _____

Facebook:

Best time to post: Saturdays @ noon (EST)
Post 3-1: 3 posts for engagement, 1 for promotion
Try to post 2-3 times per week
Post photos – they get the most "likes"
Use your logo for your picture photo, change your timeline photo regularly

Try to take five minutes each day to check your Facebook business page. Engage with people – respond! Address any negative comments or concerns. Thank those who post positive comments or reviews. Answer questions.

Track your work here:

_____

_____

_____

_____

_____

_____

_____

_____

_____

_____

15 Minutes

Twitter:

Tweet midweek & weekends around 12 & 6pm (EST)
Tweet 3-1: 3 tweets for engagement, 1 for promotion
Try to tweet every other day
Retweet and hashtag
Consider using coupons (twtqpon.com)

Try to take five minutes each day to tweet. Find local people to follow (customers, media, etc.) – use the search feature to find people in your zip code, city, county and industry. Consider connecting your Twitter account with your Facebook account so Tweets appear on FB.
Track your work here:

_____

_____

_____

_____

_____

_____

_____

_____

_____

_____

20 Minutes   Date: _____

LinkedIn:

LinkedIn is about connections – fill out your
profile and company page thoroughly
Try to update at least weekly
Spotlight products and services
Ask for recommendations and reciprocate
Join groups and engage in discussions
Make connections carefully – ask
customers/clients if you can connect

Try to take five minutes each day to update.
There is a little checkbox at the bottom of
your "Share an update" box that copies
everything you share with your
Connections on Twitter. Use #in in Tweets
to have them appear on LinkedIn.
Track your work here:

_____
_____
_____
_____
_____
_____
_____
_____
_____
_____

25 Minutes

Pinterest:

Pin original material or repin daily if possible
Best times are lunchtime, dinner time,
Saturday morning
Follow others and their boards
Pin/repin things that compliment your brand
and season
Link pins back to your website or include that
info in the pin

Try to take five minutes each day to pin.
Add pin descriptions. It can be up to 500
characters and should include SEO-friendly
keywords. You can also use hashtags
(sparingly).

Track your work here:

_____

_____

_____

_____

_____

_____

_____

_____

_____

_____

30 Minutes

Periscope:

Periscope is a live video-streaming app on your phone that posts your videos (for 24 hours) on Twitter and Periscope
Periscope followers are notified of your broadcasts and notification is posted to your Twitter feed
Use daily if possible for spontaneous (very short) broadcasts

Try to take five minutes each day to broadcast. Viewers can ask questions (you can respond) and give love (boosts your ratings). Broadcast anything! Engage!

Track your work here:

_____
_____
_____
_____
_____
_____
_____
_____
_____
_____
_____

Thank you for buying this book!

If you liked this book, please leave a review on Amazon!

If you didn't like this book, please email me at socialmediabytheminute@gmail.com and tell me why!

Laura

www.socialmediabytheminute.com

www.ingramcontent.com/pod-product-compliance
Lightning Source LLC
Chambersburg PA
CBHW050509210326
41521CB00011B/2381